Dream Date

A Musical

Kevin Dowsett

A Samuel French Acting Edition

SAMUELFRENCH-LONDON.CO.UK
SAMUELFRENCH.COM

Copyright © 1985 by Kevin Dowsett
All Rights Reserved

DREAM DATE is fully protected under the copyright laws of the British Commonwealth, including Canada, the United States of America, and all other countries of the Copyright Union. All rights, including professional and amateur stage productions, recitation, lecturing, public reading, motion picture, radio broadcasting, television and the rights of translation into foreign languages are strictly reserved.

ISBN 978-0-573-08065-4

www.samuelfrench-london.co.uk

www.samuelfrench.com

For Amateur Production Enquiries

United Kingdom and World excluding North America

plays@SamuelFrench-London.co.uk

020 7255 4302/01

Each title is subject to availability from Samuel French,

depending upon country of performance.

CAUTION: Professional and amateur producers are hereby warned that *DREAM DATE* is subject to a licensing fee. Publication of this play does not imply availability for performance. Both amateurs and professionals considering a production are strongly advised to apply to the appropriate agent before starting rehearsals, advertising, or booking a theatre. A licensing fee must be paid whether the title is presented for charity or gain and whether or not admission is charged.

The professional rights in this play are controlled by Samuel French Ltd, 52 Fitzroy Street, London, W1T 5JR.

No one shall make any changes in this title for the purpose of production. No part of this book may be reproduced, stored in a retrieval system, or transmitted in any form, by any means, now known or yet to be invented, including mechanical, electronic, photocopying, recording, videotaping, or otherwise, without the prior written permission of the publisher. No one shall upload this title, or part of this title, to any social media websites.

The right of Kevin Dowsett to be identified as author of this work has been asserted by him in accordance with Section 77 of the Copyright, Designs and Patents Act 1988

CHARACTERS

Kathy
Kathy's Mother
Miss Dalton, her teacher
Raymond Cooper ⎫
Mike Bradshaw ⎬ messenger boys for the magazine *Dream Date*
Tony Atkinson ⎭
The Editor
Mr Atwell, the sub-editor
Jobsworth, the commissionaire
Carole, a supermarket checkout girl
Lynda
Dave ⎫
Sally ⎬ characters in Double Love Trouble
Julie ⎭
A Pop Star
An Agony Aunt
A Shampoo Advertisement Girl
The Magazine: letter readers, pin-ups, fashion models, office workers, advertisements, horoscope readers and adoring fans

DREAM DATE

First presented at Eastlea School, London E16 in April, 1984, by pupils of Eastlea School. It was subsequently performed at the Theatre Royal, Stratford East with the following cast of characters:

Kathy	Sasha Lyons
Kathy's Mother	Jayne Williams
Miss Dalton, her teacher	Bridget Ball
Raymond Cooper	John Vann
Mike Bradshaw	Gary Rogers
Tony Atkinson	Roy Francis
The Editor	Beverley Mussington
Mr Atwell, the sub-editor	Kevin Dowsett
Jobsworth, the commissionaire	Alan Clasper
Carole, a supermarket checkout girl	Janie Robinson
Lynda	Jackie Thomas
Dave	Kevin Crumbie/Paul Finn
Sally	Jackie Thomas/Angela Mesher
Julie	Janie Robinson/Cordelia Barker
A Pop Star	Kevin Crumbie
An Agony Aunt	Cordelia Barker
A Shampoo Advertisement Girl	Marianne Harney
The Magazine	Cordelia Barker, Kevin Crumbie, Paul Finn, Roy Francis, Marianne Harney, Alison Hemmings, Janette Husbands, Angela Mesher, Janie Robinson, Gary Rogers, Danny Smith, Jackie Thomas, Susan Thomas
Body Poppers	Troy Braham, Anthony Terrelonge, Lee Wilson, Paul Williams

Directed by Kevin Dowsett
Musical direction by James Osborne
Designed by Tom Hardy

The actions takes place in and around the teenage magazine *Dream Date*

ACT I
  Scene 1 The opening
  Scene 2 Kathy's bedroom
  Scene 3 The *Dream Date* offices
  Scene 4 A classroom
  Scene 5 Ray's front room
  Scene 6 The locker room at *Dream Date*
  Scene 7 Telephone call
  Scene 8 Double Love Trouble

ACT II
  Scene 1 Centrefold
  Scene 2 Outside the cinema
  Scene 3 Problem page
  Scene 4 The front entrance to *Dream Date*
  Scene 5 Somewhere else!
  Scene 6 The closing

Time—the present

MUSICAL NUMBERS

ACT I
1	The Opening	Chorus
2	Editorial	Editor and Chorus
3	Change Of Scene	Instrumental
4	Kathy's Song	Kathy and Chorus
5	Deodorant	Chorus
6	Pandora's Beauty Box	Chorus
7	Underscore	Instrumental
8	You're A Girl So It's OK	The Editor
9	Horoscope	Horoscope Girl
10	Horoscope (Reprise)	Horoscope Girl
11A, 11B, 11C	Double Love Trouble	Chorus
12	Weave Our Dreams	Kathy and Ray
13	True Love	Chorus

ACT II
14	Centrefold	Pop Fans
15	Momentum Paradisum	Pop Star
16	Jingle (i)	Chorus
17	Love Says Goodbye	Agony Aunt and Assistants
18	Jingle (ii)	Shampoo Advertisement Girl
19	Blind Alleys	Ray and Kathy
20	Nostalgia's Not What It Used To Be	Mr Atwell
21	Kathy's Song (Reprise)	Kathy
22	The Closing	Chorus

The vocal score is available separately from Samuel French Ltd. Full orchestral parts for *Dream Date* are also available, please contact Samuel French Ltd for further details.

AUTHOR'S NOTE

Dream Date is about contrast. The contrast between fantasy and reality; between what things are and what things seem to be. The audience is constantly invited to make comparisons by seeing one idea played off against another. The magazine, for example, should dominate the stage throughout, emphasizing its influence over people's lives.

The function of the Chorus is vital as they represent the pages of the magazine brought to life. They should sparkle in order to point up the irony of the narrow vision they project. To create this background commentary, it would help if one or two members of the chorus were to pose behind the action of each reality scene. It might also be helpful to stress the link between the Chorus songs and the surrounding scenes.

The magazine cover should be filled with the title DREAM DATE and a boy's face, in the style of *Oh Boy!* or *My Guy*. It needs to be at least 8 feet × 5 feet and hinged with another piece of the same size so that it can be freestanding when opened out into a V-shape. A wooden frame with a hardboard covering should be strong enough to hold it together. If the Pop Star's eyes are to light up for the final number, the wiring must be connected before one of the sides is attached. Visually the inner page can be a mixture of the magazine's ingredients. A glance through any teenage romance comic will provide plenty of ideas.

Kathy's bedroom can also be built from a wooden framework covered with hardboard. Again it can be freestanding if hinged so that there is a longer side of 6 feet with two shorter flaps of 3 feet. This will also make for compact storage backstage. For the *Dream Date* offices the bedroom can simply be turned round and the other side painted a plain office colour. A fire extinguisher attached to this wall could be enough to suggest the setting. The *Dream Date* front entrance is a little more complicated and needs to look imposing. Two thin stage flats, hinged with stretched muslin doors could convert into a doorway. When lit, muslin can give a glass-like appearance.

Costumes for the Chorus need to be bright and very fashionable. Magazines freely "borrow" different styles for their layouts and this should be borne in mind. Each Chorus entrance should have a different style. Anything goes! Ideas can be found from the window displays of any chic boutique. Colour is important and different combinations are fun. Each of the Chorus could wear their own colour from head to toe or the whole Chorus could look uniform with one colour. Double Love Trouble could work well merely in shades of black, white and grey. A Commissionaire's uniform can be hired from The Corps of Commissionaires, 3 Crane Court, Fetter Lane, London EC4. The Corps are so helpful that they will even supply the correct medal ribbons for Aden and Cyprus!

Lighting can also play a part in distinguishing fantasy from reality. Flat, white lighting could suffice for reality whilst anything off-beat could characterize fantasy. Unusual gels, follow spots or lighting from beneath can be very effective whilst flashboxes, disco lights, mirror balls and smoke machines can create a wonderful atmosphere if money is available.

ACT I*
Scene 1

The opening

No. 1 The Opening

The Curtain *rises to reveal an empty stage in darkness. As the Lights fade up, an enormous front cover of the magazine* DREAM DATE *is seen. The music changes tempo and the Chorus enter as fashion models "selling" the magazine and sing*

Chorus Leave all your cares behind,
Take us and you will find
Secret love, and a guy to melt your heart.

Put on the style right here,
Buy all the latest gear,
Wear it right and he'll give his love to you.

Dream Date, ready and waiting,
Dream Date, anticipating,
Lips parted, hearts beating in time.
Dream Date, sweet days of summer,
Dream Date, this guy's a stunner,
Full story, true love and romance,
If you take the chance.

The headlines are shouted by single voices

Ba ba ba ba ba ba Gorgeous Double Pin-Up!
Ba ba ba ba ba ba You Need Help We've Got It!
Ba ba ba ba ba ba ba ba Sensational Star Attraction!
Ba ba ba ba ba ba Exclusive Interview In-Depth Probe!
Ba ba ba ba ba ba Everything You Need To Know About Boys!
Ba ba ba ba ba ba ba ba ba.

Dream Date, the thrill you are missing,
Dream Date, when you're not kissing,
Just wait for that gaze in his eyes.
Dream Date, don't mind the weather,
Dream Date, when you're together,
This promise, two hearts and one mind.
(*Yelling*) Take a look inside!

---

*N.B. Paragraph 3 on page ii of this Acting Edition regarding photocopying and video-recording should be carefully read.

With a flash the magazine opens into a double-page spread revealing a colourful selection of contents. A seductive dance takes place while some of the Chorus face the magazine

>Soon you will make a splash.
>You're gonna make your match,
>Use a bait that will make him want to bite.
>When all your hopes are lost,
>Keep all your fingers crossed,
>Here's the mag for the guy to change your life.
>Dream Date you're on the rampage,
>Dream Date turn up your ampage.
>You've guessed it, sparks fly when you meet.
>Dream Date, don't keep your distance,
>Dream Date, circuit resistance.
>Keep searching, you'll find Mister Right.
>It could be tonight!

The Chorus pose for a big finish, then run to their positions

The Editor enters. She is a fashionable, dynamic lady in her twenties who smiles a lot

The following scene brings to life the Contents Page, the Chorus reacting with almost religious fervour

Editor Hi there! My name's Jackie.
Chorus Hi Jackie!
Editor I'm your friendly editor, but I don't hit too many 'eads!

The Chorus laugh uncontrollably until she suddenly stops them

How have you been since last week?
Chorus Fab, great, etcetera.
Editor Now I don't usually take anything Debbie says seriously but when she called me fatso the other day I weighed myself and found I was half a stone overweight!
Chorus (*amazed*) Half a stone overweight!
Editor I've spent a miserable week eating nothing but lettuce and reading Debbie's vast library of diet books—and now I understand why she is so bad tempered all the time!
Chorus Wow!
Editor Have you got any funny diet stories? Why not send them along to me?
Boys What a great idea!
Girls Get into shape, mate!
Editor Time for Letterline.
Chorus Drop us a line! Drop us a line! Drop us a line!
1st Girl Hi!
Chorus Hi!
1st Girl I work in a greengrocer's shop on Saturdays, and the other day I

Act I, Scene 1 3

was arranging some apples on the stand, when this gorgeous guy I'd fancied for ages sauntered past and grinned at me. "This is my lucky day," I thought happily to myself. Thinking he'd noticed me at long last, I grinned back at him. Then I suddenly found out why he was grinning. Clutched in my hand was the sign I was about to put on the apples. It read "Cheap but tasty"! Tina from Coventry.
Chorus How embarrassing, Tina from Coventry!
Editor Cover Up and Curl Up!
2nd Girl Hi!
Chorus Hi!
2nd Girl (*very enthusiastically*) The weather was sunny and I decided to try and get a tan. I stretched out in the garden reading my *Dream Date*—

The Chorus smile at the audience

—and before long I fell asleep. When I woke up a couple of hours later, I was delighted to see I'd already started turning brown all over—except my tummy. My *Dream Date*—

The Chorus smile at the audience

—had fallen over my tum and I had a big white patch! Carol, Southgate.
Chorus Better luck next time, Carol!
Editor Next!
3rd Girl Hi!
Chorus Hi!
3rd Girl I was taking my three year old brother out for a walk when I bumped into a mate of mine from school. "I think your bruv's going to be quite a dish when he grows up," she said, looking at him. After we'd left her I noticed my brother was looking really cheesed off. "What's wrong?" I asked him. "It's not fair," he replied. "I don't want to be a dish when I grow up, I want to be a policeman!" Mary, Aberdeen.
Editor He's going to cop it!
Chorus Groan!
Editor Letter of the Week!
Chorus Da-dar.
4th Girl Hi!
Chorus Hi!
4th Girl I met up with a friend I hadn't seen for ages and we had a good old natter catching up on all our news. "Is your sis still going out with the same fella?" I asked. "You mean the one with the long nose?" she replied. "No, she broke it off!" It conjures up quite a picture ...
Chorus Doesn't it?
4th Girl Jane, Swansea.

No. 2 Editorial

Editor What else have we got?
Chorus More!
Editor Much—
Chorus —more!

Editor All about?
Chorus Fashion.
Editor The latest low down on luscious lips.
Chorus Plus!
Girl True love stories.
Girl How to find a fella.
Girl What to do to keep him.
Chorus Plus!
Girl Cartoons.
Girl Crossword.
Girl Your Horoscope.
Chorus And!
Girl This week's special officer.
Editor A double-page pin-up.

A male Pin-Up enters, stripped to the waist. He breaks into a smile

Chorus This week's pin-up and his story,
  Every bit is hunky-dory.
Two Girls (*screaming, running to him*) See that body, what a face
  Bet you'd love to take my place.

The male Pin-Up exits

Chorus And so much more ...
Editor Your problems—
Chorus —and—
Editor —advice. Is your guy giving you a bad time? Well, follow this little plan:

Girl	One
Girl (*singing*)	Doesn't really matter.
Editor	Two
Girl	It won't last forever.
Editor	Three
Girl	Go and see a doctor.
Editor	Four
Girl	Try to tell your mother.
Editor	Five
Girl	Dare yourself to do it.
Editor	Six
Girl	Boys have problems too.

Editor (*speaking*) Yes, folks, we're here to help you. If you've got a problem about anything we wanna know about it. 'Cos a problem shared is a problem halved, OK? We're your best friend.

Chorus (*singing*)
  Doesn't really matter.
  It won't last forever.
  Go and see a doctor.
  Dare yourself to do it.
  Boys have problems too.

Yes, the friend you can turn to. But most of all we give you:

Act I, Scene 2   5

Chorus (*whispering*) Love.

Pause

Editor Countdown time.

The girls run to take positions as if they are in a race, then adopt cheerleader poses

Girls   Two-four-six-eight.
              There is no more time to wait.
              Three-five-seven-nine.
              Isn't it about the time?
              Find a fella, don't be slow,
              Dream Date's here so off we go!

   The Editor and Girls exit

Some of the Chorus run around the stage and adopt statuesque "model" poses which they hold throughout Scene 2

Fade to Black-out

No. 3 Change Of Scene

SCENE 2

The Lights come up to reveal Kathy sitting on her bed, behind which is a wall of pop-star posters

Mother Kathy?
Kathy Yes, Mum?
Mother Mind if we have a chat?

They smile at each other. Her Mother sits on the bed

   How was school today?
Kathy Fine.
Mother Any plans for tonight?
Kathy No.

Pause

Mother I hope you don't think I'm poking my nose in.
Kathy Don't be silly, Mum.
Mother I want you to enjoy yourself while you're young. Your dad and I didn't have the same chances when we were young. We want you to have the things we couldn't. It's only natural.
Kathy I'm happy as I am, Mum.
Mother Your dad and I aren't strict with you and we know we can trust you not to get into any trouble—you're a sensible girl.
Kathy Oh Mum!

Mother It's just that, well . . . I can't help thinking you don't get out of the house much.
Kathy I go out occasionally.
Mother You know what I mean, Kathy. When do you ever go out to a club or get dressed up for a disco? How often do you bring friends home?
Kathy I'm all *right*, Mum.
Mother Instead of that you sit up here every night on your own, playing those records and staring at those silly posters. (*She pauses*)

The Chorus changes its position

We think you should be going out and making new friends, meeting people, enjoying yourself.
Kathy Honest, Mum, I'm happy on my own.

Pause

Mother Are you sure everything's all right at school?
Kathy Mum, I'm perfectly all right, there's nothing wrong with me. I just prefer being on my own.
Mother When I was your age I was always out at parties, meeting people, having a good time. We shared our fun, we didn't shut ourselves away, love.

Pause

You're young now, but it doesn't last for ever you know. In a few years you might not be able to please yourself what you do.
Kathy Look, Mum. I want to do things in my own way. I don't want to be told what to do all the time.
Mother All right, love, but you know we're always here to talk things over. (*She rises*)
Kathy Mum. (*She moves to her and squeezes her arm*) Thanks.

They smile

Mother exits

Kathy sighs and sits on the bed. She finds her diary

No. 4 Kathy's Song

(*Speaking*) Thursday the Twenty-fourth. Read *Dream Date* before breakfast. Shepherd's pie at school. Ugh! Got B+ in History. Walked home with Janice. (*She sings*)
        Wonder if I'll find
        Someone like me,
        Able to show me how to see.
        Girls are so helpless
        Why can't we try to see what we need
        All he has to be is wise, strong, young, bold, fair, clean, cool.
Chorus   Doesn't really matter.
        It won't last forever.

Act I, Scene 3   7

| | Go and see a doctor.
| | Try to tell your mother.
| | Dare yourself to do it.
| | Boys have problems too.
| **Kathy** | Sooner or later
| | When he appears
| | I know he will calm my fears.
| | He won't get lonely
| | Or waste his time with tears in his eyes.
| | All he has to be is wise, strong, young, bold, fair, clean, cool.
| **Chorus** | Doesn't really matter.
| | It won't last forever.
| | Go and see a doctor.
| | Try to tell your mother.
| | Dare yourself to do it.
| | Boys have problems too.
| **Kathy** | He'd share every part of me,
| | Know where to look for the heart of me,
| | Keep secrets, share hidden thoughts,
| | Most of all, keep our love true.

Kathy and the Chorus exit

The end of the song allows for the scene change. Fade to Black-out

SCENE 3

The Dream Date *offices*

An Office Girl enters, wearing a short skirt. Ray follows her, smiling

Girl Wait here, please.

Raymond grins at her and she smiles back

The Girl leaves

Ray watches her go. Chewing, he looks around to see if anyone is coming. He straightens his tie, fiddles with his cuffs, whistles and looks at his watch

Mr Atwell, the sub-editor, enters. He is in his late fifties and is a stickler of the "old school". He speaks very precisely

Mr Atwell Don't slouch, lad.

Ray straightens

Your name Cooper?

Ray smiles and nods

Right! Let's get one or two things straight from the start. I run a tight ship here—a place for everything and everything in its place, and that includes

you. I presume you came along with a few expectations this morning didn't you? You thought it was going to be challenging, exciting, interesting even, didn't you?
Ray No.
Mr Atwell Did you say something?

Ray looks disgruntled but says nothing, stops chewing and shifts his weight from foot to foot. During the following he opens his mouth wider and wider

A job that you thought could accommodate your cheery personality no doubt. Where you could impress people with your wit, intelligence and qualities of leadership. Let's get this straight from the start. This office is not an extension of school. This is the big wide world. You have got to realize that you are on the bottom rung of a very long ladder—a very long ladder—and you will have to learn to know your place on that ladder and bow and scrape a bit if you want to start climbing it. (*He looks at him*) What are you gawping at, lad?
Ray (*coming to his senses*) Er. Nothing.
Mr Atwell I hope we're not going to have trouble with you. The previous occupant of your post frankly did not come up to the mark. I trust you will be an improvement, laddie.
Ray I'll do my best, sir.
Mr Atwell (*regarding him with evident distaste*) Well that remains to be seen. The first lesson I like my new boys to realize is that they are very small fishes in a very large pond. Personal appearance!
Ray (*surprised*) Pardon, sir?
Mr Atwell Personal appearance. (*As if explaining to a small child*) What you are like on the outside. It matters, lad, and don't believe anyone who tells you otherwise. For instance, your tie.
Ray My tie?
Mr Atwell Your tie.
Ray What about it, sir?
Mr Atwell It doesn't come up to the required standard, sonny. Tomorrow I shall expect a different one. (*He flicks the tie out*)
Ray Yes, sir.
Mr Atwell Along with cleaner fingernails, an ironed shirt, pressed trousers and (*getting closer*) more closer attention to personal hygiene arrangements.
Ray Do you mean I smell, sir?
Mr Atwell Are you being cheeky, lad?
Ray No, sir.
Mr Atwell There's plenty more where you came from you know. There's a long queue of youth outside those walls prepared to cut off its right arm to come and work here and do as it's told. Do you understand that? Scrupulousness is the name of the game, lad. If you can't be scrupulous then there is little point pretending that we are speaking the same language.

Mr Atwell waits for a reply but none is forthcoming

Act I, Scene 3

Now listen. Your part in this giant enterprise is small but vital. Whenever one of the staff shouts out "Boy" or "Message" or in some regrettable cases your first name, you approach the desk, collect the memorandum, fold it and transport it with your person, taking care not to collide with any third party. This is done as promptly, I repeat promptly, as possible. The yellow copy comes to my office and the pink one, if it is included, goes downstairs for filing. The recipient of the said memorandum frequently requires a return in which case you do the same procedure in reverse. In a nutshell, that is your job. A cog which keeps the main wheel turning. The secret of good business is effective communication and I am sure you appreciate the part you play in this process.

Ray Do we get a tea-break, sir?

Mr Atwell When you've got the cradle marks off your backside, sonny, that's the time you can enquire into the intricacies of peripheral matters. Any *relevant* questions?

Ray About the pink copy, sir?

Mr Atwell I'm not explaining it again. If you are too lazy to listen carefully you'll have to get someone else to explain it to you. I've wasted enough time on you as it is. If you have any further questions my assistant will help you. Oh and one more thing. I feel it incumbent upon me to say this. Just because the magazine is called *Dream Date* don't imagine that it entitles you to spend half your time conversing with the girls in the typing pool. We've all got our jobs to do.

Mr Atwell exits

Ray (*gasping*) Blimey! What the hell's a cradle mark—I didn't even know I had one of them! (*He starts chewing again*)

Mr Atwell (*off*) Don't stand there on sentry duty, lad, there's work to be done!

Ray Yes, sir. He didn't even tell me his name.

Ray exits

The Lights cross fade as

The Chorus enter with deodorant spray cans and sing

No. 5 Deodorant

Chorus Do you have sticky stains on clothes,
Up above, even down below?
Lend an ear, listen when we say
Here's the thing, use it every day.
So take this tip you'll be pleased
If you will stand up and squeeze deodorant, deodorant.

Slimy stink, we think you'll agree
Indicates lack of pedigree.
Open up all your filthy pores
Atomize any smell of yours.

Solo	And that's why sweat prevention Ought to be the convention deodorant, deodorant. Under there, daily spruce as well Otherwise sap begins to swell. Little squirt then you feel so fresh Sinking in, sanitize that flesh. Avail yourself religiously To this it's delicious.
Chorus	Deodorant, deodorant. Tst! Tst! Tst! Tst! Tst! Tst!
Solo	Back in time, 'Lizabeth the First, Of the lot, she was quite the worst, Never thought she would ever bathe, Courtiers found it best to wave. Particularly useless I bet she never used this.
Chorus	Deodorant, deodorant.
Solo (*speaking*)	In his bath Archimedes sat, Won'dring why, water's where it's at. It was then, just as he crouched down Sniffed the air and it made him frown. That's why he said "Eureka— I reek as well so seek a"
Chorus (*singing*)	Deodorant, deodorant. By reaching your early teens You're ready to take this Authoritive Oracle's advice. An anti-stain formula—that's Protective and odour free— Try this anti-perspirant advice. If you want to attract a man To be sure buy this friendly can Drive him wild, make his senses reel And you'll have extra sex appeal. It should be clear as crystal, Gesticulate with this tool, Deodorant, deodorant, deodorant, deodorant, Deodorant, deodorant, deodorant, deodorant. (*Spraying the audience*) Tst! Tst! Tst!

The Chorus exit

The Lights fade to Black-out

Scene 4

A classroom

The Lights come up on Kathy and Miss Dalton, a patronizing teacher, who is seated at a desk

Miss Dalton You deliberately spoilt your work. Why? I could understand it if you weren't getting anywhere with it but it happened to be the best thing you've done all term.

Kathy is silent

We're not going to talk, is that it? You surprise me, Kathy, I really thought you were above this sort of behaviour!
Kathy I'm sorry, miss, I ripped the picture up because I was angry. I didn't mean to offend you.
Miss Dalton What's wrong, Kathy? You used to be so popular with your class, they hardly speak to you now.
Kathy Don't you go on at me as well, miss!
Miss Dalton I'm sorry, but when someone as keen and intelligent as you loses interest it worries me. Is there anything I can do to help? (*Pause*) Come on, you don't want me to spend half an hour dragging it out of you.
Kathy It's them.
Miss Dalton I thought as much. What have you done to them?
Kathy Nothing. I just don't go around with them like I used to that's all.
Miss Dalton Why?
Kathy They're always talking about being different but basically they all want to be the same. They're terrified of being the odd one out. They all wear the same things, talk about the same things and do the same things. It's not what I want.
Miss Dalton You don't like the girls in your class?
Kathy They're all right, I've just outgrown them. Look how they complain about having to wear the same things at school. Then as soon as they are out of the gates they rush out and buy the same clothes and end up looking exact copies of each other. They're scared stiff of being different. If they knew how pathetic they looked.
Miss Dalton You look down on them?
Kathy *Dream Date* said yesterday "We're all different and we have to be ourselves, not just part of the wallpaper". Well how can you be yourself if you're busy pretending to be someone else?
Miss Dalton *Dream Date* knows best does it?
Kathy I'm not giving up what I think to fit in with them. Either they accept me as I am or they don't accept me at all.
Miss Dalton Aren't you being a bit arrogant? It's all very well being yourself but shouldn't you accept them for what *they* are?
Kathy And be part of the wallpaper?

Pause

Miss Dalton Have they got boyfriends?

Kathy Have they? You should see the kind of boys they hang around with. Well I'm not interested. I'm not a piece of meat in a butcher's shop.

Miss Dalton That's going a bit far isn't it?

Kathy You want to see them on a Friday night, miss. The full make-up, the clothes, the hair, you wouldn't know them. Some of them are living for the day when they get engaged, it's all they talk about. They know how old they will be, what house and furniture they'll get and how many kids they want. It's like getting a husband from a mail order catalogue.

Miss Dalton Do you mind being left alone by the others?

Kathy It upsets me sometimes, miss, but I'm happy with my own thoughts, I really am.

Miss Dalton I understand, Kathy. But I can't say I agree with you. You can't go on shutting out other people for ever. There are people like yourself. Sorry, this is sounding like a party political broadcast on behalf of the being sensible party.

Kathy That's OK, miss, that's what you are. I'd better be going to French.

Miss Dalton Yes, well remember what I said. There are people around like yourself if you take the trouble to look for them.

Kathy moves to exit

Kathy Is that why you never got married, miss?

Kathy exits

The Lights cross fade as

The Girls of the Chorus enter wearing dressing-gowns and pose with various forms of make-up. The Boys enter looking as macho as possible. They sing

No. 6 Pandora's Beauty Box

Girls Remember that the key to life is make-up
That box of beauty hides the real you.
Disclosure would expose the softness we girls feel inside.
So masquerade.

Boys This boy prefers a girl who takes trouble with her outside
Dressed up to kill she gets all the looks and adds to my style,
Don't you see, it's for me?

Girls Cosmetic lacquer adds that certain something
Maintains an air of mystery and poise.
Art and Nature working side by side will catch that man.
So masquerade.

Boys You girls should always take up some time to put on your face
I may complain but I don't mind waiting here all the same,
Don't you see, it's for me?

Girls Sophistication marks your fatal fault, girl,
So draw the curtains when you feel inclined.
Assemble in your mind the part you think you ought to play.
And masquerade.

Boys There are a few unfortunate souls not fit to be seen.

Act I, Scene 5

I wonder why they don't cover up their hideous skin,
Don't you see, it's for me?

The Chorus exit

Black-out

SCENE 5

Ray's front room

The Lights come up on a standard lamp and a settee on which is Ray's ironed shirt

Ray and Carole enter. She is wearing the latest fashion and a lot of makeup. She is vigorously filing her nails

Carole Then Foster walks in and you should have seen the look on Adele's face. Well to cut a long story short he told her to go and repack all the tins of baked beans and she said "That's not my job, I'm only supposed to be on the till". He went so red I thought he was going to explode or have a fit or something. (*She giggles*) And she was standing there as calm as you like as though butter wouldn't melt in her mouth. And he said, "I've had just about enough of you girls, you drive me up the wall, if you're not fiddling the tills you're finding ways to annoy me when you should be working. I'm going to get the manager down here right away." (*She giggles*) Well, what could he say 'cos he knew Adele had caught him in the stores late one night with that woman from the fish counter. So off he storms and hides out the back pretending to see the manager and who should walk in the door but the manager. Serves him right though, saying those things about us.

Ray lets out an enormous yawn

Are you listening, Ray?
Ray Oh yeah.
Carole Well after that, when he came back we were all laughing ...
Ray (*looking at his watch*) What time did you say you had to be in tonight?
Carole Eleven, why?
Ray Nothing. (*Pause, he yawns again*)
Carole Anyway, Foster had had enough by then.
Ray (*yawning*) Oh God.
Carole Is anything the matter, Ray?
Ray Well since you mention it there is something on my mind.
Carole Tell me then. Like you say, we should share all our thoughts.

No. 7 Underscore

Ray I've been giving this a fair bit of thought over the past few days. The point is this, Sandra, sorry I mean, Carole. The point is this, how long have we been going out? Three weeks? Well you know how it is, a bloke

like me doesn't like to feel restricted does he? You see I've got this need to relate positively to the world. I can't stand predictable outcomes. Know what I mean, Sal? Carole, I mean. Sorry. Life is a preordinated pattern, an endless arrangement if you like, of beginnings and endings. As the bible has it, a door slams shut and somewhere else a window opens. Or as my old man puts it, when you're learning to ride a bike, any rusty heap'll do to learn on but when you know what you're doing, get a good 'un. That's life as they say, Esther. Sorry. (*He mouths "Carole"*) Well to summarise, recrimination being the last thing on my mind I feel that relationshipwise we have passed the zenith of compatibility, Carole.
Carole (*sarcastically*) Thank you. (*She thinks for a bit*) You what?
Ray I don't want to go out with you any more.

She starts a giggle which develops into a laugh

Did I say something amusing?
Carole Ha ha ha.
Ray I don't think you understand, love, I'm giving you the brush off.
Carole (*laughing again*) Don't be silly, Ray.
Ray It's the truth.

Pause

Carole (*giggling*) You're having me on.
Ray No I'm not—look I'll spell it out for you if you like. (*He gets down on his knees*) Carole, I no longer wish to continue going out with you.
Carole (*laughing*) Get up, you fool.
Ray Give me strength. Look, you stupid idiot, this is it.
Carole What's it?
Ray Us. You and me.
Carole What do you mean?
Ray Oh God. Us. Going out together no more. (*Pointing to her*) You. (*Pointing to himself*) Me. No go out together anymore.

Carole starts giggling again then stops suddenly, she is not sure anymore whether he is joking

Oh I think the penny is beginning to drop.
Carole You mean?
Ray Yes I mean.
Carole This is it?
Ray This is it. Finis. Kaput. The end.
Carole You're not joking at all.
Ray No.

She starts laughing again but halfway through it turns into floods of tears

Oh blimey. Look can you keep it down a bit, please? I should think they can hear you at the other end of the street.

She cries even louder

Blow your nose, you're making your mascara run, Deb.

Act I, Scene 5   15

Carole (*through her tears*) Carole.
Ray (*feebly*) Just a joke.

She blows her nose on her handkerchief

That's better. We don't want the neighbours round do we?

She starts again

Oh no. Look if I get you a Coke will you promise to shut up?

She stops

Thank God for that!

She starts again

Look, love, I don't want to get tied down at my age, do I?
Carole There's someone else, isn't there?
Ray Scout's honour.
Carole There is, there must be. I'll break every bone in her body.
Ray Look, will you believe me? I don't want to go out with you any more that's all.

Pause

Carole You think I'm ugly.
Ray No I don't, you look all right.
Carole Thank you.
Ray Don't mention it. I just think it's time for a change.
Carole I hate you! (*She stamps on his foot*)
Ray Charming.
Carole You said you loved me.
Ray Well we all say things on the spur of the moment. I meant it when I said it.
Carole But it's supposed to be forever.
Ray Now don't be silly. If I feel something, I say it. If I don't, I don't.
Carole You only said it 'cos it suited your plans.
Ray Now don't be like that, you'll only hurt yourself. Look on the bright side and you'll get over it, there's plenty more pebbles on the beach.
Carole (*tearfully*) I don't want the other pebbles, I want you.
Ray Well you can't have me. Flip me, I'm getting sick of all this. First you make all that palarva and now look what you've done, cried all over me shirt for work tomorrow. My mum's just ironed that!
Carole Good.

Pause

Ray I hope we can still be friends. (*Pause*) We can, can't we. I mean, if we meet in the street you won't ignore me will you?
Carole I don't know, I'll have to see.
Ray That's better.
Carole Right then I'd better be going.
Ray I suppose so.

Carole Don't worry, I'll find my own way out, we wouldn't want the neighbours to see us would we?
Ray OK.

She moves

Oh, there's just one more thing.
Carole (*turning*) Yes?
Ray Have you got Angela Burrows' telephone number? It's for a mate of mine, he wants to go out with her.

Ray exits. Carole exits as the Lights cross fade to the Editor who enters with a sleazy walk which changes into an aggressive, karate-kicking stance as she sings

No. 8 You're A Girl So It's OK

Editor Have you found a guy
Who gives you the eye, but
Then is rather shy?
What you need is help, so
Go and help yourself!
Get in line, sister,
Say "You're mine, mister!"
Here's a way to get started, just follow him home.
No necessity to tap his phone.
Make the best of your time, boldly ring his bell.
As he opens the door, you can open up the war.

Now launch the attack,
Hold those shoulders back, and
Give his face a slap.
His astonishment,
Will be heaven sent.
Now's the time, sweetie,
Make those eyes weepy!
Take the bull by the horns tell him you need no flag,
Or your get-up-and-go soon will sag,
All you want from him now is a time and place,
If he doesn't fall for these,
You could get down on your knees.

If he gives you flak,
You could always pack, your
Aphrodisiac.
With a sidelong glance,
Press home your advance.
Mobilize, just a
Tiny blockbuster.
Knuckle your duster

Act I, Scene 6   17

    Watch that guy rust away
    You're a girl so it's OK!

The Editor exits

Black-out

Scene 6

The locker room at the Dream Date *offices*

The Lights come up on Mike, Tony and Ray, who are all dressed in suits. Mike is priggish—a sort of Atwell in the making

Mike I don't mind a bit of fun but if they don't find out who put that stink bomb in the staff loo then we're all under suspicion.
Ray I don't know what you're talking about, old boy.
Mike Oh yes you do. Don't act the innocent with me, I've been here longer than you.
Ray You don't give the orders around here. If Atwell walked in now you'd be jumping around like a frog with diarrohea.
Tony You wouldn't be accusing us, would you, Michael?
Ray Not without evidence I hope?
Mike You know I haven't got any proof.
Tony Well then, you must be careful what you say.
Ray The laws on slander are very precise.
Mike I don't understand you, Tony, you were all right before Ray arrived but now you've changed.
Ray He's got a different pair of underpants on!
Mike You'll be laughing on the other side of your face before long.
Tony Is that supposed to be a threat?
Mike Take it how you like, I've got my future career to think of.
Ray Excuse me, Mr Atwell, would you like me to go to the loo for you? (*He turns on Mike*) Nobody pushes me around, Bradshaw.
Mike I've a good mind to speak to Atwell tonight. You've given me more trouble in two weeks than I've had in the past three years.
Tony I shouldn't, mate, not if you want to save up for that deposit.
Mike Wait till you get engaged and see how you like it.
Ray I'm not that stupid, mate.
Tony Watch your blood pressure.
Mike I'm off.
Ray I knew it was something.
Mike And try to show a bit of consideration for other people.

Mike exits

Ray There he goes, engaged at nineteen, married by twenty-one, two point four kids by twenty-five. Total interests in life, paying the mortgage, doing the washing up, gardening and going to Butlin's once a year. He spends his whole life taking orders from other people and calls it responsibilities. Then when he gets the golden handshake at the age of sixty he'll wonder what the hell to do because there'll be no-one to give him orders. He'll spend all his time setting himself little targets like going down to the Post Office and collecting his pension, going on coach outings with his wife in the summer and waving at any stupid bugger who will wave back. Future prospects nil. Ask yourself, why is he still running errands after three years?

Pause

I packed her in last night.
Tony You didn't?
Ray She was cramping my style. Very understanding about it though, even gave me her best friend's telephone number.
Tony How often do you change your girls?
Ray About as often as you change your socks—twice a year.
Tony I've got to hand it to you.
Ray Soon as I see them filing their nails and putting their hair in place, I know it's only a matter of time before they start filing me and putting me in place.
Tony So who's next on the list then?
Ray Can you keep a secret?
Tony Of course.
Ray What does this stupid magazine get every week?
Tony I dunno. Adverts?
Ray Come on.
Tony Quizzes, horoscopes, letters.
Ray Ah ha.
Tony Letters?
Ray Exactly. And who are these letters from?
Tony Girls.
Ray You've got it, girls, letters from girls. Hundreds of girls pining for an understanding, handsome, modest fellar. And what is written at the top of the letter?
Tony The address?
Ray Ten out of ten!
Tony You're not going to write?
Ray What do you think I am! I look at the address, if it's not too far away I look up the telephone number. Course, you've got to be choosy, some of them are a bit young and I'm not interested in the ones writing about their spots.
Tony You can't take those letters, they're confidential. Atwell would go bananas if he found out.
Ray He's not going to find out—unless you're thinking of telling him.
Tony You must be off your head. How can you get away with a trick like that?
Ray Natural charm, son, something you'll never have. Listen to this. (*Reading a letter from Kathy*) "Dear *Dream Date*, I can't understand why

Act I, Scene 6

everyone wants me to be like everyone else. Am I silly to wait for the right boy to come along? All my friends seem to go out with any boy that asks them. Am I wrong in believing in fate and hoping that somewhere I will meet a boy who will be all my dreams?" What about that then? And there's plenty more where that came from.

Tony (*whistling*) You've got more front than Dolly Parton. What are you gonna do?

Ray Let's just say a young lady is about to be recruited into the Raymond Cooper school of charm and elegance. An interesting little course, short in duration but long in achievement!

Tony You bighead!

Ray Now don't be nasty to your Uncle Raymond otherwise he won't include you in his little scheme.

Tony No thanks, I know which letters you'd give me, I wasn't born yesterday. See you later.

Ray Not if I see you first.

Tony exits

Ray continues reading the letter

Mr Atwell enters, unseen by Ray

Mr Atwell Ah Cooper, doing a spot of overtime?

Ray (*changing his manner completely*) No, sir, just cleaning out my locker, I like to keep it tidier than the others. It takes a little longer, but it helps me to start the day with the right attitude.

Mr Atwell I wish the others had that attitude, Cooper. Now I wonder if you can help me. I'm investigating a little matter, a culprit who has perpetrated the toilet facilities with an obnoxious effluvium. Would you be able to assist me in my enquiries?

Ray You surely don't think I . . .?

Mr Atwell Certainly not, Cooper. I thought you, being a sensible lad, may have heard something of mutual benefit.

Ray Sorry, sir, I've no idea.

Mr Atwell What about your compatriots, Bradshaw and Atkinson?

Ray I wouldn't like to say.

Mr Atwell Come along, Cooper, you can tell me. Loyalty is a quality to be admired but it may do your future career no end of harm.

Ray I don't like to accuse anyone without evidence but Michael did seem in a rush to get away tonight. Said something about the last two weeks giving him more problems than he has had in the last three years. I think he thought that he was due for some promotion by now.

Mr Atwell Did he by Jove!

Ray I'm sorry, sir, I ought not to be saying this.

Mr Atwell Not at all, Cooper, it's all in strictest confidence. I shall have a word with young Mr Bradshaw tomorrow. (*He moves to exit*)

Ray Could I make a suggestion, sir?

Mr Atwell (*stopping*) Go ahead, Cooper. I like initiative.

Ray Speaking as a friend I think he's going through a bad patch at the moment. Emotional pressure perhaps. He got quite shirty with me when I tried to be friendly, but you know how it is.

Mr Atwell I do indeed. But vaulting ambition is not a particularly endearing characteristic when accompanied by malicious intent.

Ray I'd say the milk of human kindness had pretty well evaporated from some people, wouldn't you, sir?

Pause

Mr Atwell Yes, Cooper. We seem to speak the same language. In time there could be an opening somewhere for you.

Ray and Mr Atwell exit

Black-out

SCENE 7

The telephone call

The Lights come up on a small group of the Chorus. They introduce the Horoscope Girl who takes up a central position. Kathy is sitting in a chair reading Dream Date. *There is a telephone beside her*

No. 9 Horoscope

Chorus (*singing*) Stars of love will give you hope
Time for this week's horoscope.
Horoscope Girl (*speaking*) Miss Pisces. You could be in for a surprise which will make your mates green with envy. A fella may sweep you off your feet with an offer you can't refuse. This could be the best thing to happen for absolutely ages so don't play hard to get. Don't blow your chance for a whirlwind romance.

The telephone rings

Ray enters with a telephone. He and Kathy are lit in two separate areas and do not look at each other during the scene

Kathy Hello.
Ray (*official voice*) Hello, this is British Telecom. I'm testing the line, would you mind helping me?
Kathy OK.
Ray Good.
Kathy What do I have to do?
Ray Just keep talking. Can you hear me all right?
Kathy Fine.
Ray What does my voice sound like?
Kathy It sounds sort of interesting.
Ray That's very flattering, but I meant is it too loud or too soft?
Kathy Oh I'm sorry.

Ray Don't apologize, you've got an interesting voice too.

Pause

Have you got any children?
Kathy No, I'm only sixteen.
Ray I was sixteen last year.
Kathy Oh really.
Ray Do you know I've got this strange feeling that we've met before.
Kathy That's very unlikely I'm afraid.
Ray Why, I meet a lot of different people in my job.
Kathy Have you finished with the telephone?
Ray Not yet. Look, this is going to sound very silly but can you keep speaking on your own while I check the line?
Kathy What do you want me to say?
Ray Whatever you like, most people say a poem or something.
Kathy I don't know any poems.
Ray What about a nursery rhyme.
Kathy You mean like "Ba Ba Black Sheep"?
Ray That'll do fine.
Kathy Are you sure about this?
Ray Yes. Don't worry, only Busby can hear you. (*During the following, he practises "weight lifting" his end of the telephone*)
Kathy All right.
        Ba ba black sheep, have you any wool?
        Yes sir, no sir, three bags full.
        One for the master and one for the dame,
        And one for the little boy who lives down the lane.
Ray Can you do it again?
Kathy Ba ba——
Ray Thank you.
Kathy Was that all right?
Ray Fine. (*Acting shyly*) Erm. This is going to sound really corny and it's highly irregular but could I ask you a personal question?
Kathy Depends what it is.
Ray Will you come out with me?

No. 10 Horoscope (*Reprise*)

Horoscope Girl (*speaking*) Don't blow your chance for a whirlwind romance.
Ray Hello, hello are you still there? Only to tell you the truth I'm a bit shy of actually talking to someone in the flesh. It's different over the phone 'cos no-one can see me. You sound the sort of person who would listen. Say you'll come.
Kathy I don't know.
Ray Do you believe in fate?
Kathy I suppose I do.
Ray So do I. I mean here I am, day after day phoning people up when suddenly, today, I get this irresistable urge to talk to a real human being,

not just a voice on the phone. Do you know what I mean? Why today? Why you? It must be *fate*.
Kathy I suppose it must.
Ray You'll come then?
Kathy I'll have to think about it.
Ray What is there to think about? Either you will or you won't. I tell you what. I'll wait outside the Town Hall at eight o'clock and if you think I look like a crank or something then you can walk right past and I'll be none the wiser, OK?

Pause

Kathy All right. Yes, I'll come.
Ray See you later then, real human being.
Kathy See you later, Busby.

Everyone exits

Black-out

Scene 8

Double Love Trouble

The Lights come up on the Editor

Editor Double Love Trouble!

The Chorus enter with a square frame, within which Sally and Dave (and later, Julie), who are wearing expressionless masks, move like robots. Their voices are provided by three more actors who stand watching the frame, if possible speaking with microphones. This allows thoughts to be whispered. They are melodramatic in both movement and voice. Sally carries a book

No. 11A Double Love Trouble (i)

At the library

Sally Wow! He looks a hunk. (*She drops her book*) Gosh I've dropped my book.
Dave Allow me.
Sally Oh thanks (he's dishy).
Dave I'm Dave.
Sally I-I'm Sally.
Dave Fancy us meeting here.
Sally In the library?
Dave No, in the Romance section.

They both look up at a sign which reads ROMANCE

Sally Oh, so we are. I hadn't noticed that.
Dave It must be a sign.

Act I, Scene 8   23

They turn and look again

Would you like a date?
Sally (Gosh, look at those gorgeous eyes. I think I'm falling for him in a big way.) Oh, look at the title of my book!
Dave (*reading*) *Never Say No.* C'mon you've got to say yes now.
Sally OK, Dave. When?
Dave No time like the present, Sal.
Sally (*mustn't seem too eager*) I'll have to think about it. OK! Oh boy!

The Chorus freeze in position as the action switches to

Ray and Kathy who enter on their date, wheeling a motorbike

Ray (*trying to sound modest*) Yes it goes OK. I've got the two videos on one side and the hi-fi and the Space Invaders on the other. Then the bed folds up into the wall and the colour telly and the juke box swing round to cover the space.
Kathy So where do you keep your record collection?
Ray There's another room for that—you walk into it, just like a library really.
Kathy You're so lucky.
Ray Oh, I dunno, you get used to it. I mean, if you've always had these things you never stop to think about it.
Kathy (*after a pause*) Why didn't you bring your car tonight?
Ray Me dad's car went in for a service so I said he could borrow mine. Well he does lend me the Jag sometimes. Anyway, I might be getting rid of it soon.
Kathy Too expensive?
Ray No I'm bored with it, it's no fun anymore. I fancy getting a Porsche like my sister.
Kathy Your sister's got a Porsche?
Ray Yeah, but it's two years old. A bit clapped really. I like driving but I really like stock car racing at the moment. It's a shame I'm not racing this week but you can come and watch me the week after next if you like.
Kathy Could I?
Ray Yeah sure. You know, has anyone told you you've got really smooth skin?
Kathy Oh thank you.
Ray No kidding, it was the first thing I noticed about you, that and your eyes.
Kathy My eyes?
Ray Oh yes, I always look in someone's eyes first. (*He gets closer*) They say you can tell exactly what someone is thinking by looking in their eyes.
Kathy You can? (*She backs off*)
Ray Course you can. Like right now I can tell that you quite like me because your pupils have gone all dilated.
Kathy Oh.
Ray Don't worry, I don't mind, I've seen it in other girls. It's nothing to worry about, just a bit of a giveaway if you like. Let's have a closer look.

Cor yeah, I reckon you've got Marta Hari eyes, you know about her, don't you?
Kathy I thought you were shy?

Pause

Ray Pardon?
Kathy Shy. On the phone, you said.
Ray (*thinking quickly*) Well I am, usually very shy you know. But, you've made me feel so relaxed, I didn't even realize. Usually I find it difficult to talk to people because I get so embarrassed.
Kathy How long have you worked at British Telecom?
Ray Oh, since I left school. (*Pause*) I expect you're wondering why someone like me works in such an ordinary job?
Kathy No I wasn't.
Ray Well my dad wants me to pick up the trade from the bottom, learn the hard way. Then in a year or so when he makes me a manager I'll have experience of shop-floor work. As they say (*in Atwell's voice*) "the secret of good business is effective communication".
Kathy Oh I see.
Ray Anyway, we've only just met, you don't want to talk about boring old me all the time. I bet you think I'm a right show off. Let's talk about you.

Kathy smiles at him

What was your last boyfriend like?
Kathy My last *boyfriend*?
Ray Yes.
Kathy What was he like?
Ray Yes. What was his name?
Kathy Er . . . his name?
Ray (*knowing the answer*) Yes . . . You have had a boyfriend before?
Kathy (*too quickly*) Oh yes, of course.
Ray Surely you remember his name, or have there been so many?
Kathy (*unconvincingly*) Er . . . it was Peter, yes that's right, Peter.
Ray Oh, how long did you go out?
Kathy Er . . . let's see . . . it must have been six months.
Ray That's a long time.
Kathy No, I might be wrong, it could have been three weeks.
Ray Oh. You'll have to tell me about it.

Kathy and Ray freeze as the action jumps back to the frame

Editor Meanwhile at the cinema

No. 11B Double Love Trouble (ii)

Dave and Sally crouch behind a cut-out of some cinema seats

Dave Great film, isn't it?
Sally Yeah. (Who's watching the film?)
Dave I wouldn't want to be anywhere else.

Act I, Scene 8

Sally I knew from the start we'd end up together. I don't know if you believe in love at first sight, but I do.
Dave Me too!

She moves to him, he turns away

Editor But!

Pause, dramatic chord

Sally What—what's wrong, Dave, why did you turn away?
Dave Did I? Oh, I didn't mean to, it's nothing. (*He puts his arm around her*)
Editor Sally was falling more in love every minute.
Sally I'm so glad I found you, Dave.
Dave Me too, Sal.

Dave exits

Editor As the days passed ...

Julie enters the frame

Sally He's a real dream, Julie, I never guessed it could be so good.
Julie Mmm. I—I don't know how to put this, Sal, but I've *got* to tell you.
Sally Tell me what, Jul?
Julie I wouldn't say anything, but you're a friend. You see, it's Dave.
Sally Dave?
Julie Yes Dave.
Sally You don't mean ...

Pause, dramatic chord

Julie Yes, he's two-timing you.
Sally No, no! It can't be true.
Julie I'm sorry to be the one to tell you, but you had to know.
Sally Thanks for telling me, Jul.
Julie What are you going to do?
Sally I'll have to see him and sort out the truth. Oh gosh what a mess!

The Chorus freeze as the action jumps back to Kathy and Ray

Kathy I'm sorry.
Ray I don't know what's the matter with you. You give all the signs with your clothes and make-up and all that, then when anyone comes within a yard of you, you run a mile. (*Pause*) Have I got the plague or something?
Kathy No.
Ray I'm relieved to hear it. Other girls aren't so fussy.
Kathy You're not quite what I expected.
Ray What do you want me to do, have a head transplant?
Kathy I hoped you'd be yourself.

Pause

Ray What the hell's that supposed to mean?
Kathy I haven't met you yet—all I've met is a chat up routine.

Ray Do me a favour. That's the way it goes—a bit of chat then when you respond, a little cuddle and wallop! It's a warm up to the main event.
Kathy Is it?
Ray Rather watch telly would you?
Kathy Yes.
Ray Oh great! What's so special about you?
Kathy I'm being myself, that's what's special.
Ray Oh and I'm not I suppose.
Kathy You probably think you are. I'm sorry, I think I'd better walk home on my own.
Ray Here, hold your horses a minute. I wanna know how come you're yourself and somehow I'm not.
Kathy You really want me to tell you?
Ray Yeah go on, tell me something I don't already know.
Kathy The truth hurts.
Ray I'm big enough, I can take it.

Pause

Kathy All girls have an idea of their perfect fella, right?
Ray If you say so.
Kathy I'm not starry eyed about it. He doesn't have to be tall, dark and handsome with blue eyes and a scar on his cheek. He doesn't have to have pots of money and be a part-time sex symbol and rock star. I don't expect Simon le Bon to come charging along on a white horse and sweep me off my feet so we can live happily ever after. He could be an ordinary bloke. It'd be nice if he was good-looking but even nicer if he said what he thought and let me do the same. Someone who accepts me for what I am.
Ray Oh right, I'll be off now then.
Kathy Oh no you don't. I really thought when you phoned me up that here was a chance. A chance in a million to speak to someone who would listen. Someone who didn't pretend to know all the answers.
Ray I see—I disappointed you then.
Kathy Instead of that I got "Anyone ever told you you've got really smooth skin". Smooth skin! Marta Hari eyes! I was supposed to be impressed was I? Then when I didn't respond like all the other girls I get told I'm fussy. Look here, Martin Kemp, I'm nobody's main event, got it?

Pause

Ray You can't blame me for doing what's natural. I chatted you up because that's what it's all about.
Kathy You didn't ask *me*.
Ray Oh I get it, I've got to go round saying, "Excuse me, darling, would you mind if I chatted you up right now if you've got nothing else planned". I'm not a bloody mind-reader you know; nobody's complained before.
Kathy Does that make it right for *me*?

Pause

Act I, Scene 8   27

Ray I've got a reputation to keep up.
Kathy Your reputation matters more than mine does it?

Pause

Ray I've never met a girl like you before, you've got an answer for everything.
Kathy Does it worry you?
Ray I dunno. It takes a bit of getting used to, I'll have to think about it.
Kathy What is there to think about? Either you know or you don't. You know, you've got lovely eyes.
Ray Do you really think so?
Kathy No.

Dave enters the frame as Julie leaves

Ray and Kathy freeze as the action jumps back to the frame

Editor Later at Dave's house.

No. 11C Double Love Trouble (iii)

Dave What's wrong, Sal?
Sally There's something I *must* ask you.
Dave What's on your mind, Sal?
Sally Are you going out with someone behind my back?
Dave W-who told you?
Sally So it's true. Oh Dave, how could you do this to me? I thought you loved me.
Dave You must tell me who told you.
Sally My mate Julie—she said everyone knew you already had a girl. Everyone that is, except me.
Dave Believe me, there is a reason.
Editor Dave's words made Sally stop and think.
Sally I think you'd better tell me everything, Dave.
Dave It's like this, Sal. Julie told you right.
Sally You mean you *are* going out with someone else?
Dave No.
Sally What else could it mean?
Dave Julie was right to tell you, but it was only half true.
Sally I don't understand, Dave.
Dave I guess I'll have to tell you everything. Promise not to be angry with me?
Sally I'll try.
Dave I wanted everyone to know about this girl so I spread it all over town. Julie must have heard it.
Sally Why didn't you tell me the truth, Dave?
Dave That's just the point, Sal. There *is* no girl at all. You see, I'm in a group but I wanted to keep it a secret. So to cover my nights out I invented the girl.
Sally Oh Dave, you didn't lie at all.

Dave I couldn't tell you before, but now our record has got to number one it's OK.
Sally I knew I'd seen you before.
Dave I had to be sure you liked me for the right reasons, and you did.
Sally I was sure it would turn out all right in the end.
Editor Sally was happy now she knew the truth.
Dave How about a pizza to celebrate before our record goes out of the charts?
Sally You'll always be number one with me, Dave.
Dave Do you mean that, Sal?
Editor Dave found his answer in Sally's kiss.

Dave and Sally kiss then they, the Editor and the Chorus, exit

The action jumps back to Ray and Kathy

Kathy I lied to you.
Ray You did?
Kathy About having a boyfriend. (*Pause*) I've never been out with a boy in my life. (*Pause*) I lied about my age too. I'm not sixteen, I'm fifteen and a half. Do you mind?
Ray Do I mind? For a girl on her first date you're not doing badly.
Kathy You don't mind about me lying then?
Ray No. (*Pause*) I did too.
Kathy About?
Ray Just about everything.
Kathy I don't mind.
Ray You don't?
Kathy Why should I? Did you think I'd be impressed?
Ray Most girls are.
Kathy I'm different.
Ray You're that all right.
Kathy I wrote to a magazine about it.
Ray Which one?
Kathy I doubt if you've heard of it, it's called *Dream Date*.
Ray Oh.
Kathy I wanted to know what was wrong in being different.
Ray What did they say?
Kathy I didn't get a reply.
Ray I wouldn't have thought you needed their advice. (*Pause*)

The music for No. 12 starts

(*Changing his tactics*) I could say anything to you, couldn't I?
Kathy Anything.
Ray OK, I'll tell you something. I put on an act because that's what people expect me to do.
Kathy You don't always have to do what people expect.

Pause

Ray That's right.

Act I, Scene 8

Kathy By living a lie you can't grow inside, because all your efforts are going in the wrong direction. I got that out of *Dream Date*.
Ray Oh yeah.
Kathy It's true enough. You've got to find happiness inside yourself. Cheat and you'll lose it.
Ray *Dream Date*, correct?
Kathy Correct. (*Pause*)
Ray Yeah you've talked me round. Why not be honest with people? I've never stopped to think about it before. Why lie just because they do?
Kathy Right!
Ray I'm not afraid to be different.
Kathy Why should you be?

Pause

Ray I like you, Kathy. You've got a brain and you're not afraid to use it. I don't need to pretend with you.

No. 12 Weave Our Dreams

Kathy   Suddenly you see
(*singing*)   Superficiality
                   Buttons up, embroiders you.
                   No need to pretend
                   If you see that honesty
                   Wears its heart upon its sleeve.
                   I don't wanna live a lie, my simplicity
                   Doesn't feel the need of eternal vanity.
                   But then
                   Can't I find a way to keep curiosity?
                   Help me understand
                   How to interweave my dreams with you.

Ray (*speaking*) I act big because it makes me seem important. But it's all a big cover up, I'm not really like that. Most girls I meet are stupid so I treat them badly. Do you know the thing that really amazes me—they don't mind being walked all over and treated like a door-mat? Some of them enjoy it—(*pause*)—but you make me think—(*pause*)—you know, the difference between a fantasy and a fallacy.

Kathy   Fantasies and fallacies, this is what I am.
(*singing*)   Every night I spent alone thinking 'bout a man.
                   But now
                   Jealousy won't bother me, I don't give a damn.
                   Help me understand.
                   Weave your dreams when we're alone.
                   Weave them close into my own.

Ray and Kathy sit closer together and appear to be talking to each other, before they exit hand in hand

No. 13 True Love

The Chorus enter as disco dancers with a mixture of latest dances and special effects. Good dancers perform solo spots or work in groups

Chorus (*singing*)	He's a real cool cat, And he's found someone to purr with. It's a sure fire thing You can put your money on TRUE LOVE. Every girl needs love 'Cos it makes her life complete, yeah! If you search you'll find That he's searching for the same TRUE LOVE. Turn the lights down low If you're feeling really smoochy. It's the time to show In your lips he'll always find TRUE LOVE. He's a real cool cat, And he's found someone to purr with. It's a sure fire thing You can put your money on TRUE LOVE. Every girl needs love 'Cos it makes her life complete, yeah! If you search you'll find That he's searching for the same TRUE LOVE. TRUE LOVE. TRUE LOVE. (*Shouting*) Yeah!

CURTAIN

ACT II

Scene 1

Centrefold

There are two crowd control barriers between the magazine and the audience

No. 14 Centrefold

When the Curtain *rises, the stage is empty, lit from behind and filled with smoke. Pop Fans enter, dressed as schoolgirls and each carrying a large photograph of the Pop Star. At first their manner is friendly but later they become more aggressive*

Pop Fans (*singing*)	I've got every record you've made My scrapbook is full. I know everything about you Your face fills my wall.
Solo	I know that you are married, I don't care if our love Won't lead there, we've Got something more.
Pop Fans	Keeping you near my pillow You set me on fire. No-one knows how long I've waited To be set on fire. Ah! Ah! Other girls had better watch out If you come this way. I would find a reason somehow So you'd want to stay.

There is an air of excitement as the rest of the Chorus enter to await the arrival of the Pop Star. Jobsworth, the uniformed commissionaire, enters

(*Half-whispering*)	I could be the one, I could be the one, I could be the one girl. If he would agree, he could follow me, I could be the girl who will Make a perfect love, make a perfect love, make a perfect lover.
(*Singing*)	Put your hand on his heart and I'll tear you apart in a flash.

(*Half-whispering*)   I could be the one, I could be the one, I could be the one girl,
If he could agree, he could follow me, I could be the girl who will
Make a perfect love, make a perfect love, make a perfect lover.

Jobsworth pushes them back

(*Singing*)   Don't you try to get tough, we've got enough troubles without you.

The excitement mounts as the Fans push their way to the front of the crowd. Jobsworth is on crowd control duty

The Pop Star enters. He is the archetype; sullen and aloof

Loud screams greet his arrival

No. 15 Momentum Paradisum

Pop Star   Do you want the adoration from identikit
(*singing*)   Buzzing round a light sensation of one hundred watt?
A pubescent, packaged body,
Effervescent, adolescent me?
Endlessly this repetition passes through each day
Private thoughts conflict with public image, every way!
Gratified desire numbed this brain
Only function apathy won't drain.
Erotic invitation oh
My directive is suggestive
Rip me off
Rip me off.
Endlessly this repetition passes through each day
Private thoughts conflict with public image, every way!
Gratified desire numbed this brain
Only function apathy won't drain.
Momentum paradisum oh
Seduction interruption
Is the age
It's a stage.
Momentum paradisum oh.
Momentum paradisum oh.
Momentum paradisum oh.
Momentum paradisum oh.

The Pop Fans reach out with their hands, but the Pop Star is hustled away. Some scream and give chase. The Pop Fans exit

Black-out

Scene 2

Outside the cinema

The Lights come up on Kathy and Lynda, wearing their best clothes, standing behind a sign which reads: SCREEN 3 Queue Here. *There is much looking at watches and glancing left and right*

Kathy Waiting for a fella?
Lynda Yeah.
Kathy Me too. He's not usually late.
Lynda I thought he'd be here by now. If he doesn't come in a minute, we're gonna miss the feature.
Kathy Snap!
Lynda It's only our second date.
Kathy Oh.
Lynda (*proudly*) Said he'd be bringing his sister's Porsche.
Kathy What's his name?
Lynda Ray.

Pause

Kathy He sounds nice. How'd you meet him?
Lynda You won't believe it, straight out of a magazine story. He was working for British Telecom and he phoned me up.
Kathy Oh yes.
Lynda Said he liked my voice and would I go out with him?
Kathy Isn't that nice?
Lynda Yeah and he's a real dream. He really knows how to treat a girl.
Kathy Sounds terrific.
Lynda It's what you might call a whirlwind romance, we've really fallen for each other. It's early days yet but you know, wow!
Kathy Dynamite, eh?
Lynda Yeah.
Kathy You don't mind telling me?
Lynda No. To tell you the truth it's nice to have someone to tell. My mum thinks I'm round my mate's house. She'd throw a wobbler if she knew I was going out with a bloke who drives a Porsche.
Kathy I bet.
Lynda Ray's so funny.
Kathy Makes you laugh does he?
Lynda All the time.
Kathy Does he talk about himself?
Lynda Never stops. I think he's on the rebound though. The way he goes on about this girl who mucked him about. Bitch! (*Proudly*) We were saying how important honesty is in a relationship, don't you agree?
Kathy (*sarcastically*) Oh yes.
Lynda Apparently this girl couldn't be honest. I expect she was a bit immature, using him for his money and that.

Kathy Probably.
Lynda I told him to forget her and be honest with me. (*She laughs*) I've never been so honest with anyone on a first date. (*Pause*) What's your fella like?
Kathy He just finished with me.
Lynda But you said you were waiting...
Kathy (*smiling*) No. it's all over.
Lynda Oh I *am* sorry.
Kathy I shouldn't bother. I've got a feeling that Porsche is somewhere else tonight being honest to someone else on their first date.
Lynda Oh no. He said to make sure I was *here* because he had something to tell me.

Pause

Kathy It must have been embarrassing singing over the phone.
Lynda (*laughing*) Yes. (*Pause*) How did *you* know?
Kathy You're not the only one who's been honest with Raymond.

Pause

Lynda I'll break his bloody neck if I ever see him again.

Lynda exits

Black-out. Kathy remains on stage for the beginning of the next scene

SCENE 3

Problem page

A small group from the Chorus enter and sing

No. 16 Jingle (i)

Chorus
We are here to help you,
Feelings we can gauge.
Send us all your troubles,
To your problem page!

An Agony Aunt and her three Assistants enter. They look like Diana Ross and the Supremes and move and sound a lot like them too. During the following song, Kathy exits

No. 17 Love Says Goodbye

Lead
Heard he called you up on the telephone.
Feeling bad but he had to tell you
There was someone new,
She was not like you.
Now each day drifts by in a lonely haze.
Staring out on memories you made.

Act II, Scene 3

If you're really sore,
Don't want any more.
Love says goodbye,
Telling you it's your turn to cry, baby.
Love says goodbye.
Listen to me, don't wonder why, baby.
Only way to get over him
Is to look for another guy.
Whenever love says goodbye,
Your turn to cry, baby.

Saw him walking out with another girl.
Holding hands and laughing together
Like he used to do,
All those times with you.
If he knew the pain that is in your heart,
Watching him give her the love you had.
Now you are apart
Mend that broken heart.
Love says goodbye,
Telling you it's your turn to cry, baby.
Love says goodbye.
Listen to me don't wonder why, baby.
Only one way to get over him
Is to look for another guy.
Whenever love says goodbye
Your turn to cry, baby.

(*Speaking*) Did the tears trickle down your face as you watched him close that door and walk out of your life? Did you think happiness had gone forever as that love flame flickered and died? But, you know, thinking 'bout those times won't bring him back. Baby, you've got to build a new life for yourself and heal those wounds of love. You've got to face up to facts and say . . .

(*Singing*)   Love says goodbye,
Telling you it's your turn to cry, baby.
Love says goodbye.
Listen to me don't wonder why, baby.
Only way to get over him
Is to look for another guy.
Whenever love says goodbye
Your turn to cry, baby.

Everyone exits

Black-out

Scene 4

Outside the Dream Date *offices*

The front entrance is impressive with double doors containing the magazine's logo

The Lights come up on Jobsworth, the uniformed commissionaire, who stands in the doorway

Kathy enters

Jobsworth Where are you going, miss?
Kathy In there.
Jobsworth Have you got an appointment?
Kathy No.
Jobsworth I'm sorry, nobody comes in here without an appointment.
Kathy But I must.
Jobsworth Come along, miss, it's more than my job's worth to let you in there.
Kathy You don't understand. It's very important.
Jobsworth It's you that doesn't seem to understand. It's my job to stop people like you getting in without an appointment. We can't go letting any Tom, Dick or Harry start wandering in, now can we?
Kathy Please let me in?
Jobsworth (*getting angry*) You don't seem to understand the Queen's English. Unless you want to feel the toe of my boot I'd advise you to be on your way.
Kathy I'll give you money.
Jobsworth Oh dear me no, I've got responsibilities. I can't go on accepting bribes, now can I? I've been in this business a long time. Twenty-five years I've guarded these portals since coming out of the Regular Army. I've faced the height of Beatlemania, I've single-handedly quelled a near riot of Donny Osmond fans, on one occasion I held back the entire Bristol branch of the Duran Duran fan club.
Kathy There's only one of me, I'm not exactly a crowd, am I?
Jobsworth Trying to be clever are we? I know all the tricks so you're wasting your time. Oh yes! You'll be surprised what some of them think of— forged passes, letters of introduction. It's always the same, especially when one of these popular groups is making an appearance. But I pride myself in knowing that no-one has got past me yet.
Kathy Do all the big groups come here then?
Jobsworth Oh yes we've had them all here.
Kathy Bet someone's got in.
Jobsworth They've tried. A favourite trick used to be over the roof from an adjacent building until we set up an alarm system. The Bay City Rollers, ever heard of them? No, I suppose they were before your time. Right vicious lot, their fans put me in hospital for three weeks, little so and so's. Oh yes!

Act II, Scene 4   37

Kathy I'm not going to hurt anyone.
Jobsworth Maybe not, miss, but I've got my prestige to consider. My standing as a uniformed commissionaire. That's a very important element of my kind of work. I've got to have respect. If I had to go back to my little wife in Tufnell Park and tell her my security had been breached, I wouldn't be able to look her in the eye. Oh yes, the pride in a job well done, the tidiness of having enforced the rule of law, is the satisfaction that keeps me going. Like that screaming mob of girls we had in here the other day, what was it they called themsleves, Spastic Ballet? Oh yes! I don't know who thinks these names up. Come on, we've all got our jobs to do.

Kathy tries to push him past but he is too quick for her. He rapidly has her arm in an armlock

Oh yes! Oh yes! A bit of physical force now is it? Talking to you wasn't good enough. That's the trouble with you youngsters, you can't take no for an answer. Well now you'll have to wait until I call up a uniformed policeman to eject you officially. I thought you were going to be nice and gentle. Thought I could trust you. It just shows you can't be too careful.

She continues to struggle

Kathy Let go of me!
Jobsworth Dignity at all times. You thought an old chap like me couldn't hold his own, didn't you? Well, young lady, I'll have you know that I served in Aden and Cyprus, unarmed-combat instructor.
Kathy I'm sorry. I did it on the spur of the moment.
Jobsworth Well if you know what's good for you the next thing you'll do on the spur of the moment is to clear off out of it before I call up reinforcements. Look, here's the editor. Don't for gawd's sake cause any trouble in front of her, go on now, clear off!

The Editor enters

Morning, ma'am. (*He salutes*)
Editor Morning.
Kathy Excuse me, can I speak to you, please?

Jobsworth quietly fumes

I need some advice, the boy I was going out with——
Editor I'm sorry, the magazine cannot involve itself on a personal level with individual problems.
Kathy But the problem page says "We're here to help you" and gives this address.
Editor Of course it does. That is the address for written correspondence. If you read it properly you will also notice it says at the bottom of the page that problems can only be dealt with through the Letters Page. Sorry, but I've got a meeting to go to.
Kathy So you're not interested in my problem?

Editor Not just at this moment, love — send in a letter and we'll see what we can do.
Kathy That's not good enough, I've come a long way to get here.
Editor OK. What's the matter? Boyfriend getting you down? Pregnant? See your doctor. Speak to your mother.
Kathy You couldn't care less.
Editor Not particularly. Look, love, whatever it is, in a couple of years time you'll look back and think "Wasn't I silly", now can I get by, please?

Kathy snatches a folder from under the Editor's arm and runs to one side. The Editor motions Jobsworth to keep still

Give me that folder, it doesn't belong to you.
Kathy (*reading*) "Monthly sales figures, Shampoo."
Editor Give me that folder.
Kathy (*holding the folder in the air*) I want some advice first. Some individual advice on a personal level.
Editor I haven't got time now. I'll find someone to come out and speak to you.
Kathy Not if you don't want me to tell the world the "Monthly Sales Figures, Shampoo".
Editor (*looking round for passers-by*) All right!
Kathy I've read *Dream Date* since I was twelve. Every week.

The Editor looks at her watch

Don't look at your watch. I take some of it with a pinch of salt. I'm not stupid but I believed there was a fella somewhere for *me*. All I had to do was wait. Well he came along. Just what I was hoping for. Everything he said was a lie.
Editor Oh dear, what a shame! Shall I cancel today while we all have a little cry into our pillows? Who do you think you are?
Kathy (*bitterly*) I believed in my world. I was strong in it.
Editor Do you think you are the only girl in the world who this happens to? We get hundreds of tear-stained letters every week, pouring out their grubby little romances. It's time you grew up and looked around. Why should you have the monopoly on sorrow?
Kathy I told him everything. All my secrets.
Editor More fool you to put all your trust in someone else. If you're stupid enough to live in a dream world then you'll get hurt.
Kathy But you told me to live that way, with your happy endings and all that sensible advice.
Editor What the hell do you expect? We're running a business not the local branch of the Samaritans. Do you want stories with boys picking their noses and girls having unwanted babies? Is that what you want? The truth mag? Do you want us to tell our readers that we think they're mostly stupid. They're going to marry someone who is equally stupid and after a couple of years shouting at each other produce a kid who will be the same. Do you want us to tell people that a life of unremitting boredom awaits them in the factory and in the home? Because that is what it's like for a lot

of people. Is that what you want; because you're the only person in the world who would buy it.
Kathy But you're selling lies!
Editor Do you think I don't know that? If life's so bloody miserable with no prospect of it getting better, people need to escape. We're here to help them. Don't you worry, we know exactly where we fit in—we know what you girls want, we've spent a lot of money finding out and we make damn sure we give it to you. If you don't like it, go and find your own answers. There's your advice, now give the folder back.

Kathy opens the folder and begins to read

No. 18 Jingle (ii)

The Shampoo Advertisement Girl enters. She carries a bottle of "New Lustre" shampoo

Advertisement Girl Let's get it straight, girls, some of us suffer from a lack of self confidence. If we have a large nose or an unsightly mole on our chin then the chances are that we worry about it so much it becomes a bit of an obsession. True? Well, there's one little answer that'll leave you brimming over with confidence and wondering why you never thought of it before. Here's how. "New Lustre" by Wemgem. Create a new look. It doesn't matter whether your hair is greasy, lank and dry, or normal and unmanageable because the new, unique CL7 formula controls your hair and actually adjusts to its natural condition. So forget that little blemish and build yourself a new face and a new confidence with "New Lustre" by Wemgem. The shampoo that controls your confidence.
(*Singing*)   You owe it to yourself not to lack Lustre.

The Shampoo Advertisement Girl exits

Kathy (*reading from the folder*) "The August figures shows a distinct drop for Wemgem at the bottom end of the market." That's giving people what they want is it? That's their escape?
Editor Give me that!

A struggle develops but Kathy holds the folder over their heads

Kathy You just want a load of zombies who accept everything that's put in front of them. I see through your "keep 'em happy" dreams with your plastic people and your CL7's. You don't want people to be different—they're all the same to you. A market to make money. Well you don't get any more of mine.
Editor Oh your twenty-seven pence is going to make a lot of difference! You're only one in five thousand. Check our circulation. Who cares about you?
Kathy *I* do! You're not controlling what I think. I make my own decisions. You sell your cardboard cutie to some other stupid girl. You *sell* them the idea of a girl worshipping the ground some clod-hopping, arrogant boy walks on. 'Cos you don't get me.

Ray enters with a message for the Editor. He does not see Kathy

Ray Sorry to interrupt, urgent message from Mr Atwell. Would you like me to stay for a reply?

Pause

Editor Thank you, Raymond.

Kathy realizes who he is and throws the folder up so that the papers scatter throughout the stage. The Editor advances on Kathy

You think yourself very lucky that I'm not calling the police. Raymond, pick all those papers up immediately and bring them in, I've wasted enough time this morning.

Ray (*looking at Kathy*) Er, if you don't mind I'd rather not.
Editor I do mind, you are trying my patience, Cooper.
Ray Right away.

The Editor exits with Jobsworth

Ray begins picking up the papers

Kathy A messenger boy, that's about your level isn't it?
Ray (*nervously*) Hi.
Kathy You coward. You couldn't even tell me yourself.
Ray I'm sorry it had to be you.
Kathy Oh sure. Any more clichés while you're about it?

Pause

Everytime you try and grab a little happiness it turns out to be a load of old stinging nettles. Schoolgirl poetry, eh? Go on laugh, you might as well, you won didn't you?

Ray I'm not laughing. (*Picking up the last of the paper*) You know your trouble, Kathy, you expect everyone to come up to your standard. You tell everybody to "be themselves" but you can't handle it when their real self isn't what you wanted.
Kathy All *I* ever wanted was the truth.
Ray Oh is that all. Why don't you put an advert in *Time Out*? "Naïve girl seeks boy for totally honest relationship. No lies please." Nobody with any brain puts *anyone* before themself.
Kathy I know plenty who do.
Ray And where did it get them? Nowhere! All they've got is the satisfaction of some other idiot's gratitude. What good is that? You can't wear it. You can't eat it.
Kathy Everything's just a function to you, isn't it? It's all there to be picked up and used. You don't respect anything, it's just what *you* can get out of it!
Ray You bet! There's no time for anything else. I want it all and I want it right now.
Kathy Want what?

No. 19. Blind Alleys

Ray OK you want philosophy

Act II, Scene 4   41

(*singing*)	Life's too short to wait and see,
	Yes sir, no sir, all the way.
	Gotta get ahead
	Make it to the top.
	Before it's too late
	Before it's too late
	'Cos when you're forty you're dead
	You're mentally grey
	Hairline receding
	And nothing to say.

He gives a short swaggering dance to the music

                     The cream will rise to the top of the milk
                     It's element'ry.
                     It won't be long till I'm up there myself
                     One of the gentry.
                     It may seem rather obvious
                     One day soon others succeed us.

                     I want the status that money can buy
                     Right now believe me!
                     Gold-plated Rolls and a fancy bow-tie
                     Like on the TV.
                     Life is my university
                     No point in hands getting dirty.

                     I don't believe that it should be me
                     My responsibility
                     To indulge in misery.

Kathy   Don't you realize?
                     Don't you understand?
                     It's only a dream.
                     It's only a dream.
                     Though you think you control them,
                     These plans in your head,
                     You'll never wake up to find
                     Breakfast in bed.

Ray dances again

Ray   Expensive clothes and a holiday cruise
                     To be specific
                     Asleep all day and all night on the booze
                     In the Pacific.
                     This self-made man is coming soon,
                     The day for calling in my tune.

                     The cream will rise to the top of the milk
                     It's element'ry.
Kathy   And all your honesty is sour!

Ray	It won't be long till I'm up there myself One of the gentry
Kathy	They won't give you the power!
Both	Why is it you can't see That you're lost in a blind alley? Blind alleys lead you to nowhere Blind alleys lead you to nowhere Blind alleys lead you to nowhere Blind alleys lead you to nowhere.

Kathy If it happened *tomorrow* you'd never be satisfied.
Ray I'll find that out for myself thank you very much.
Kathy You'd wake up one day and realize it was all a lie.
Ray I'd pretend it wasn't.
Kathy And you'd make all the same mistakes as those grey-minded people—in fact you'd be *one* of them. You'd be shovelling the *same* lies down the *same* stupid throats.
Ray That's right.
Kathy It doesn't have to be like that. You don't have to swallow all that stuff, it could be different. You could be yourself. Free to have principles and stick to them instead of being told what to think.
Ray Any more advice you want to give me?
Kathy You haven't got the guts to see you've sold yourself a lie. You kid yourself, but there'll always be someone above you pushing you around, and you'll have to lick their boots for the rest of your life.

Kathy storms off

Ray is left staring after her

Mr Atwell and Jobsworth enter

Ray (*shouting after Kathy*) I might even do that!

Mr Atwell taps Ray on the shoulder

What is it? (*He turns*) Ah, Mr Atwell.
Mr Atwell Ah Cooper. Lover's tiff? Do continue.
Ray Sorry, sir.
Mr Atwell Oh sorry are we? I wondered if it had escaped your notice that you have been spending the company's time for your own nefarious activities.
Ray I'll try to see that it doesn't happen again.
Mr Atwell You'd better. In future keep your little tarts away from the office or your number will be up, matey. Are you aware how long the editor has been waiting for that document which, even now, you are dog-earing in your sweaty palms? Are you listening?

Ray is still thinking about Kathy

Ray What's that?
Mr Atwell The folder.
Ray Oh, I forgot about it.

Act II, Scene 4   43

Mr Atwell Did you? Now look here, when the editor says jump, I jump. That's what I'm paid to do, and she's waiting. I thought you knew your place, laddie. I thought you and I had a bond of understanding, a respect for the *principles* of commerce.

Pause

Ray Did you say principles?
Mr Atwell I did, lad. (*Pause*) I'm waiting.
Ray (*to the audience, as a tennis commentator with a plummy voice*) And it's a super day here, perfect conditions and the court is in first-rate form. The players have finished limbering up so we're ready to go. Atwell to serve.
Mr Atwell I beg your pardon, laddie?
Ray Fifteen love.
Mr Atwell What did you say?
Ray Nothing.
Mr Atwell I'll think we'll continue this discussion inside. (*He moves to the door*) Laddie!
Ray Thirty love. The first ace of the match.
Mr Atwell What on earth are you talking about?
Ray Net! He'll have to do better than that.
Mr Atwell (*getting angry*) Look here, sonny.
Ray (*shouting*) Fault. (*Quietly*) First service. Is he losing his touch?
Mr Atwell Laddie!
Ray Forty Love. Obviously not, that was a peach of a shot.
Mr Atwell You're going the right way about making me extremely angry!
Ray (*offhand*) Really?
Mr Atwell (*through clenched teeth*) Yes really.
Ray Forty-fifteen. Cooper's opened his account.
Mr Atwell I didn't want to mention it but Bradshaw has been to see me with certain allegations about you. Of course I was not prepared to listen, but in the light of your behaviour this afternoon I feel more inclined to hear what he has to say.

Pause

Ray (*constantly waiting for a "laddie"*) Forty-thirty. Disappointment.
Mr Atwell Yes, perhaps in the past I have been rather too lenient with you. Hardworking and useful though you have been.
Ray (*after a pause*) Deuce. Is he throwing this game away?
Mr Atwell You are making me very angry, boy.
Ray (*helpfully*) Nearly. Try laddie.
Mr Atwell Laddie?
Ray Advantage, Atwell. He seems to have sorted out his service now.
Mr Atwell What are you playing about at?
Ray And it's match point with the atmosphere very tense. (*Indicating Jobsworth*) The crowd is agog, anxiously awaiting the outcome of this tremendous struggle. Here we go then for the final point of the match. Quiet please!

Mr Atwell I'm going inside. When you've returned to your senses, Cooper, you can collect your cards and your P forty-five from personnel.
Ray And he's not going to say it! It could be all over and he was so close.
Mr Atwell Say what?
Ray (*laughing*) You know.
Mr Atwell I don't know what you're talking about.
Ray Go on. Don't be shy.
Mr Atwell Impertinence! Nobody speaks to me like that. Give me that folder. I'm not wasting any more time here.
Ray Who would have thought it, the match almost in the bag and he is crumbling before our eyes. I'll give you a clue. (*He mouths the word "Laddie"*)
Mr Atwell (*not understanding*) Lady?
Ray (*groaning*) Game, set and match to Cooper. Hard luck. Shake hands with the winner. (*He holds out his hand*) I'm not your laddie, your sonny or your matey. All right? I do not go out with little tarts. Got it? I'm not playing your game any more. I've got rid of the cradle marks off my backside as you so delicately put it and I intend to live a bit before I turn grey like you.
Mr Atwell This is my natural colour.
Ray Not your hair you fool, your brain, your attitude, your bloody ladder of success. You take your ladder and your grey suit and your required standard tie (*he flicks his tie out*) and your pink, yellow and blue slips and your "Monthly Sales Figures, Shampoo" and shove them up your personal, hygiene-arranged nose!

Ray goes to throw the papers and they cover their faces, but he changes his mind

Ray exits

(*As he goes*) Match abandoned!

Mr Atwell, clearly embarrassed, sends Jobsworth off

Jobsworth exits

Mr Atwell smartens himself up again. He sings very precisely at first but then becomes a 40s crooner

No. 20 Nostalgia's Not What It Used To Be

Mr Atwell Why is it the youngsters of today
Cannot be content with their lot?
Retrospection is frowned upon
But putting the boot in is not.

"Keep up with the Joneses" is their code.
The theory I have will expose
Namby-pamby attitudes
Leave a pile of unwashed clothes.
Long before

Act II, Scene 5

> We bowed and worshipped the altar of youth,
> I remember a man was treated
> With respect, if long in the tooth.
> The young they glance forward, we gaze back.
> Regret is the current malaise,
> Try to understand the young
> Or explain their latest craze.

The Magazine Dancers, who parade 40s fashions, and the Editor enter. There is a mirror ball effect on them

Editor (*speaking*) Fling back the forties!
Mr Atwell   Nostalgia's not what it used to be
  (*singing*)   Promotion the only desire.
> Pecking order then ruled the roost
> And nobody's purchase was hire.
> A "young generation" there was not,
> If seen or heard was in disgrace.
> We all soon became aware
> That there was a time and place.
> They forget
> We were young with star filled nights of romance.
> Days of lingering charm that promised
> A new life that love would enhance.
> But now they are all possession mad
> Dream-factory colour TV.
> I have lost the good old days
> But they won't, they won't lose me.

Everyone exits

Black-out

Scene 5

Somewhere else!

No. 21 Kathy's Song (Reprise)

The Lights come up as Kathy enters alone

Kathy   He'd know every part of me,
  (*singing*) Know where to look for the heart of me.
> Keep secrets, share hidden thoughts,
> Most of all keep our love *true*.

Ray enters carrying the folder

Ray Kathy, I did it. You should have seen his face. The old fogey was ordering me about and suddenly I couldn't do it any more. I realized he's only got power if I give it to him. I don't have to give him any respect —

my self-respect's more important. I feel so strong I could do anything. Look, I've been buggered off with the "Monthly Sales Figures, Shampoo". (*Pause*) It was all down to you, you know.
Kathy (*unenthusiastically*) Great.
Ray I thought you'd be a bit happier.
Kathy Did you?
Ray I chucked it all in for *you*.
Kathy No you didn't. You did it for yourself. Like you said, you're strong now, you won't get pushed around next time.
Ray Is that all you've got to say?
Kathy Yes.
Ray Oh.
Kathy Aren't you forgetting, you finished with me, you got a girl to tell me.
Ray Forget all that, it's different now.
Kathy No thanks, Ray, I'd rather not. I learnt a lot from you and I'll say hello if I see you about but I'd rather wait for someone else to come along.
Ray Still wishful thinking, eh?
Kathy There's nothing wishful about looking for happiness, it means being a bit more selective that's all.
Ray Oh I get it. It's all right for me to face up to the truth but not for you.
Kathy Think what you like.
Ray I will, thank you very much. It's all very well having a dream but you can't live inside your head. You'll end up staring at the walls wondering why nobody wants to know you.
Kathy Maybe.
Ray I'm not a saint. No-one is. You've got to take me as I am with all my faults.
Kathy I don't have to take you at all.
Ray You're looking for a dream that doesn't exist, any more than that crappy magazine, it's all in the mind. You've got to live in the real world and be happy while you can.
Kathy I'll keep looking thank you. I want my happiness to last.

Mike enters

Ray Oh look who it isn't. The new crawler. Come for the "Monthly Sales Figures, Dandruff" no doubt. (*To Kathy*) What was it like, throwing this up?
Kathy Very liberating.
Ray Shall I?
Kathy Why not?

Ray throws up the folder

Ray Pick up that lot, laddie!
Mike (*after a pause*) Mr Atwell!

Mike runs off

Kathy Strong, eh?
Ray Yeah.

Act II, Scene 6

Kathy You'll never get that Porsche now.
Ray I've got something more important.
Kathy I'm not going out with you, Ray. Understand?
Ray If that's what you want.
Kathy That's what I want. (*She moves to exit*)
Ray I don't like sad endings.
Kathy (*smiling*) Well don't make a habit of them.

Kathy exits. Ray thinks for a moment before he exits in a different direction

Black-out

Scene 6

The closing

The Chorus and the Editor enter in darkness and stand with their backs to the audience. They turn gradually as the Lights come up and they sing

No. 22 Stop! Look! Listen To Us!

Chorus	La la la etc.
	All good things come to
	An end, we're telling you.
	So make the most of this
	Short but happy life.
	Time is the loser
	Step out, pull on your shoes.
	A weekly magazine
	Will help you kick off the blues
	La la la etc.
Editor	It's nearing the time to escape the next
	First try out your wings before you head West.
Chorus	Stop! Look! Listen to us!
	Magazines throughout your teens.
	Kids, mums, any age between
	We feed everyone's dreams.
	Next issue Thursday
	Reserve without delay
	Arriving soon
	Only twenty-seven pence.
	Fantastic faces
	Will help your hopes revive
	The latest trend this year,
	It will bring your love alive.
	La la la la etc.
Editor	No need to upset your reality
	Especially as those dreams remain free.

Chorus   Stop! Look! Listen to us!
                    Magazines throughout your teens,
                    Kids, mums, any age between,
                    We feed everyone's dreams.

The Chorus retreat back to the magazine and close it. The Lights fade and they stand either side of the cover. The "eyes" of the cover face wink and then stay lit. The Chorus begin to move towards each other and then move towards the audience in a tight group, as one. They begin to repeat "Stop! Look! Listen to us!", starting as a whisper and building in intensity until they are shouting at the audience. They become very menacing. After the final "Stop!" they freeze and then smile as they sing

                    Stop! Look! Listen to us!
                    Magazines throughout your teens.
                    Kids, mums, any age between,
                    We feed everyone's dreams.
                    Stop! Look! Listen to us!
                    Magazines throughout your teens.
                    Kids, mums, any age between,
                    We feed everyone's dreams.
                    Everyone's dreams.

During the final pose, some of the Chorus are reading next week's issue of Dream Date

                              CURTAIN

FURNITURE AND PROPERTY LIST

Please see the Author's Note on page vii.

ACT I

Scene 1

On stage: Magazine

Scene 2

Set: Bedroom wall covered with posters
Bed. *On it:* pillow and bedspread

Personal: **Kathy:** diary

Scene 3

Strike: Bedroom wall, bed and contents

Set: Office wall with the extinguisher

Personal: **Ray:** wristwatch (worn throughout)
Mr Atwell: yellow, pink and blue slips of paper

On page 9
Strike: Office wall

Personal: **Chorus:** deodorant cans

Scene 4

Set: Table. *On it:* paper, pencils
Stool

On page 12
Strike: Stool, table and contents

Personal: **Girls' Chorus:** various cosmetics
Boys' Chorus: combs

Scene 5

Set: Settee. *On it:* **Ray**'s ironed shirt
Standard lamp

On page 16
Strike: Settee, shirt, standard lamp
Personal: **Carole:** nailfile, handbag containing handkerchief

Scene 6

Set: 3 lockers
Personal: **Tony:** yellow, pink and blue slips of paper
Ray: letter

Scene 7

Strike: 3 lockers
Set: Chair
Table. *On it:* telephone
Off stage: Telephone **(Ray)**
Personal: **Kathy:** *Dream Date* magazine
Ray: letter

Scene 8

Strike: Chair, table and telephone
Off stage: Double Love Trouble frame **(Chorus)**
Sign: ROMANCE **(Chorus)**
Motorbike **(Ray)**
Cinema seat cut-out **(Chorus)**
Personal: **Dave:** mask
Sally: mask, copy of *Never Say No*
Julie: mask

ACT II

Scene 1

On stage: Magazine
2 crowd control barriers
Personal: **Pop Fans:** large Pop Star photographs

Scene 2

Strike: 2 crowd control barriers
Set: Cinema sign: SCREEN 3 Queue Here
Personal: **Kathy:** wristwatch
Lynda: wristwatch

Scene 3

Strike: Cinema sign

Scene 4

Set: Front entrance to DREAM DATE

Personal: **Editor:** wristwatch, folder containing several sheets of typed paper
Shampoo Advert Girl: bottle of "New Lustre" by Wemgem
Ray: blue slip of paper
Mr Atwell: pink and blue slips of paper

Scene 5

Strike: Front entrance to DREAM DATE

Personal: **Ray:** folder
Mike: pink slip of paper

Scene 6

Personal: **Chorus:** copies of next week's issue of *Dream Date*

LIGHTING PLOT

Practical fittings required: standard lamp, magazine cover "eyes"
Various simple interior and exterior settings

ACT I. SCENE 1

To open: Black-out

Cue 1	**When ready** *Fade up lighting on magazine*	(Page 1)
Cue 2	**When Chorus enters** *Bring up bright colourful effect*	(Page 1)
Cue 3	**As the Editor enters** *Change to bright general lighting*	(Page 2)
Cue 4	**Chorus exits** *Fade to Black-out*	(Page 5)

ACT I. SCENE 2

To open: General interior lighting

Cue 5	**Kathy and the Chorus exit** *Fade to Black-out*	(Page 7)

ACT I. SCENE 3

To open: Bright interior lighting

Cue 6	**Ray exits** *Cross fade to the Chorus for music No. 5*	(Page 9)
Cue 7	**Chorus exits** *Fade to Black-out*	(Page 10)

ACT I. SCENE 4

To open: Bright interior lighting

Cue 8	**Kathy exits** *Cross fade to Chorus*	(Page 12)
Cue 9	**Chorus exits** *Black-out*	(Page 13)

ACT I. SCENE 5

To open: Bright interior lighting, standard lamp on

Dream Date

Cue 10	**Ray** and **Carole** exit, the **Editor** enters *Cross fade to follow spot on* **Editor**	(Page 16)
Cue 11	The **Editor** exits *Black-out*	(Page 17)

ACT I. SCENE 6

To open: Bright interior lighting

Cue 12	**Ray** and **Mr Atwell** exit *Black-out*	(Page 20)

ACT I. SCENE 7

To open: Specific lighting for music No. 9 with follow spot on **Kathy**

Cue 13	**Ray** enters *Follow spot on* **Ray**	(Page 20)
Cue 14	Everyone exits *Black-out*	(Page 22)

ACT I. SCENE 8

To open: Follow spot for **Editor**

Cue 15	**Editor:** "Double Love Trouble!" *Off beat lighting for music No. 11A*	(Page 22)
Cue 16	**Ray** and **Kathy** enter *Cross fade to general exterior lighting on* **Ray** *and* **Kathy**	(Page 23)
Cue 17	**Ray:** "You'll have to tell me about it." *Cross fade to off beat lighting for music No. 11B*	(Page 24)
Cue 18	**Sally:** "Oh gosh what a mess!" *Cross fade to general exterior lighting on* **Ray** *and* **Kathy**	(Page 25)
Cue 19	**Kathy:** "No." *Cross fade to off beat lighting for music No. 11C*	(Page 27)
Cue 20	**Dave, Sally,** the **Editor** and **Chorus** exit *Cross face to general exterior lighting on* **Ray** *and* **Kathy**	(Page 28)
Cue 21	**Ray** and **Kathy** exit hand in hand *Cross fade to special effects for music No. 13*	(Page 29)

ACT II. SCENE 1

To open: Exterior pale light from behind

Cue 22	**Pop Fans** enter *Specific lighting for music No. 14*	(Page 31)
Cue 23	**Pop Star** enters *Follow spot on* **Pop Star**	(Page 32)
Cue 24	**Pop Fans** exit *Black-out*	(Page 32)

ACT II, SCENE 2

To open: General exterior lighting

Cue 25	**Lynda** exits *Black-out*	(Page 34)

ACT II, SCENE 3

To open: Specific lighting for music No. 16

Cue 26	**Agony Aunt** and **Assistants** enter *Follow spots on* **Agony Aunt** *and* **Assistants**	(Page 34)
Cue 27	Everyone exits *Black-out*	(Page 35)

ACT II, SCENE 4

To open: General exterior lighting

Cue 28	**Shampoo Advertisement Girl** enters *Cross fade to follow spot on* **Shampoo Advertisement Girl**	(Page 39)
Cue 29	**Shampoo Advertisement Girl** exits *Cross fade back to exterior lighting*	(Page 39)
Cue 30	**Magazine Dancers** enter *Mirror ball effect on* **Dancers**	(Page 45)
Cue 31	Everyone exits *Black-out*	(Page 45)

ACT II, SCENE 5

To open: General exterior lighting

Cue 32	**Ray** exits *Black-out*	(Page 47)

ACT II, SCENE 6

To open: Black-out

Cue 33	As music No. 22 starts *Slow fade up, bringing up cover "eyes" effect*	(Page 47)
Cue 34	**Chorus** close the magazine *Fade to Black-out, leaving cover "eyes" practical on*	(Page 48)
Cue 35	As **Chorus** move towards the audience *Fade up to full general lighting*	(Page 48)

EFFECTS PLOT

ACT I

Cue 1	**Chorus:** (*yelling*) "Take a look inside!" *Flash*	(Page 1)

ACT II

Cue 2	**Horoscope Girl:** "... for a whirlwind romance." *Telephone rings*	(Page 20)
Cue 3	To open SCENE 1 *Smoke effect*	(Page 31)

www.ingramcontent.com/pod-product-compliance
Ingram Content Group UK Ltd.
Pitfield, Milton Keynes, MK11 3LW, UK
UKHW021847210426
5322IPUK00022B/520

9 780573 080654